Life On Fire

Caleb Houston

BookLeaf Publishing

India | USA | UK

Presentation by *BookLeaf Publishing*

Web: www.bookleafpub.com

E-mail: info@bookleafpub.com

ISBN: 9789363312920

First edition 2024

ACKNOWLEDGEMENT

To my wife, Danielle:

Your unwavering belief in my potential and your constant presence as a beacon of light during my darkest days have been my greatest sources of strength. As the mother of our two wonderful children, Corbin and Willow, you have shown incredible love, patience, and resilience. Thank you for always seeing the best in me, even when I struggled to see it myself. This book is as much yours as it is mine, and I am forever grateful for your endless encouragement and love.

Always & Forever,

— Caleb Houston

PREFACE

"Life On Fire" is born from the depths of my experiences, a reflection of the battles fought both on distant shores and within the confines of my own mind. As a husband, father, and US Army Veteran, my journey has been marked by moments of profound love, loss, and resilience.

In 2009, I lost my father to suicide—a loss that has forever etched itself into my being. Our relationship was complicated, marred by distance following my parents' divorce, yet his death left a wound that words can scarcely describe. This collection of poems is, in many ways, my attempt to bridge that gap, to understand and articulate the pain, confusion, and eventual healing that ensued.

My own struggles with mental health, including a suicide attempt that I was fortunate to survive, have profoundly influenced my writing. Surviving meant that my story wasn't over; it meant there was a greater purpose yet to be fulfilled. Each poem in this collection is a testament to that belief—a beacon of hope and a call for greater mental health awareness.

"Life On Fire" is not just my story; it is the story of countless veterans, fathers, sons, and individuals who wrestle with their inner demons while striving to find peace and purpose. Through these poems, I hope to offer a voice to the voiceless, to shed light on the shadows that often go unnoticed, and to foster a deeper understanding and compassion for those battling mental health issues.

May these words ignite a fire of awareness, empathy, and healing in every reader's heart.

— Caleb Houston

Who I Am

Fifteen years, a battlefield within,
Depression, anxiety, the wars I've been in.
Not one thing to blame, a storm of strife,
Each blow shaping the contours of my life.

In 2009, a gunshot stole my dad,
A distant figure, yet the loss was bad.
Left a hollow space, unfilled to this day,
A pain that words can scarcely convey.

I followed his shadow, an attempt to flee,
Rehab's walls held the broken pieces of me.
Emerging anew, but the world felt strange,
Crowds and chaos, my mind's range.

In 2010, the Army called my name,
A soldier's path, seeking unity's flame.
Mother and brother, comrades in arms,
Finally fitting in, embracing the charms.

Graduation day, a surprise to hold,
In full uniform, their presence bold.
Tears held back, formation's demand,
A man I stood, nostalgia's strand.

2015, a son's birth denied,
A father absent, my heart cried.
A cycle repeated, history's chain,
Wanting to be there, to ease the pain.

Danielle by my side, through thick and thin,
Open and ready, for life to begin.
The state's games, a prison stint,
Fighting for my blood, each moment spent.

DCF and OCS, thorns that twist,
Reigniting trauma, the hurt persists.
Two children now, our family strained,
The fight for justice, our love sustained.

Though my journey's still winding, I stand tall,
A leader for men, heeding the call.
Vindicated Veteran, my banner unfurled,
"This We'll Defend," my vow to the world.

Masterpiece of Me

Paint me as I am, in hues both dark and bright,
With every stroke of color, reveal my inner light.
The canvas tells my story, each brush a beating
heart,
A tapestry of struggles, a masterpiece of art.

Capture all my moments, the highs and lows I
face,
The joy that lights my spirit, the tears I can't
erase.
In vibrant swirls of laughter, in somber shades of
pain,
Paint me as I am, beneath the sun and rain.

Trace the lines of sorrow, that carve into my
soul,
Blend them with the triumphs, that make my
spirit whole.
For every scar and shadow, is part of who I am,
A testament to battles, and the strength that I
reclaim.

Don't hide the imperfections, the cracks within
my frame,

For in those very fissures, you'll find the deepest
flame.
In colors bold and vivid, or muted, soft, and dim,
Paint me as I am, let every layer brim.

With empathy and kindness, with understanding
eyes,
Paint me with compassion, beneath the endless
skies.
For in the strokes of honesty, in the shades of
truth and grace,
You'll see the depth of being, in this portrait of
my face.

So paint me as I am, with all my hopes and
fears,
Let the canvas echo, the music of my years.
For in the art of seeing, in the beauty of the
blend,
You'll find the human spirit, a masterpiece to
mend.

Caleb, The Conqueror

In times of struggle, remember this,
Caleb's courage, faith amiss.
A name that bears a story told,
Of facing giants, brave and bold.
"Take the land," he firmly spoke,
With strength in heart, no spirit broke.
Challenges before him, vast and grand,
Yet he stood, with a fearless stand.
Like Caleb, I face my fight,
Through shadows deep and darkest night.
These trials, heavy, wear me thin,
Yet they're placed here for a reason, within.
Each burden, pain, and hidden tear,
Is crafted by a purpose, clear.
To embody strength, to boldly stand,
To grasp my fate with steady hand.
Mental health, a silent plight,
Yet in this darkness, there's a light.
In every struggle, every scar,
A beacon shines, a guiding star.
For Caleb's name means bold and true,
A legacy that I pursue.
Through every storm and trial, I see,
A path of hope, that sets me free.
So take my hand, let's walk this way,

Through valleys deep, to brighter day.
For in this journey, we'll find the key,
To courage, strength, and victory.

Can't Afford To Quit

In this world where shadows loom,
I stand in silence, face my gloom,
Anxiety's weight, so heavy and cold,
A story of struggle, too often told.
Each day begins with a silent scream,
As dreams unravel at every seam,
My pockets empty, heart feeling light,
But burdened by an endless fight.
Child support for a distant son,
A love I'm denied, a race never won,
My time, a bargain at twenty an hour,
A cruel reflection of power.
Vermont's taxes, a merciless theft,
Leaving me with little left,
Bills stack up, a relentless tide,
Hope flickers dim, nowhere to hide.
The worry gnaws, it wears me thin,
How can I keep my family within?
My pride is bruised, my spirit torn,
I feel emasculated, weary and worn.
With every breath, I fight this test,
I push through pain, though deeply stressed,
For giving up would mean a death,
Of dreams and hope with my last breath.
But I can't surrender to the night,

Or let despair consume my fight,
For my children and my wife too,
I must endure, I must push through.
So I gather strength from the pain I've known,
In this battle, I'm not alone,
For even when the world feels untrue,
I choose to rise, to fight and pursue.

Four Quarters

In friendships' treasury, a truth is found,
"If friends were money," echoes all around,
"I'd rather have four quarters, solid and true,
Than a hundred pennies, scattered askew."

For in the realm where hearts entwine,
Quality surpasses quantity, a goldmine,
Four quarters gleam with steadfast shine,
While pennies, though many, can't align.

A single quarter, steadfast and bold,
A friend who listens, a hand to hold,
Through trials and triumphs, they stand near,
Their value cherished, forever clear.

Four quarters forge a bond so rare,
Each one precious, beyond compare,
Their worth not in numbers, but in trust,
In laughter shared and love robust.

So let the pennies jingle, countless and bright,
Yet in the heart's ledger, they dim in light,
For friendship's wealth, in its richest scenes,
Is found in four quarters, loyal and keen.

Can You Hear Me?

If Heaven had cell phones, oh, the calls I'd
make,
To whisper through the clouds, my heart to take.
Dad, can you hear me? Hold on, hold tight,
Better days are coming, there's a break in the
night.

I'd dial Aunt Mic, with her number divine,
To thank her for being my godmother, so fine.
The years we shared, the laughter, the tears,
A bond that transcended the sum of our years.

And then I'd call a friend, my wife's granddad,
Though we call him Papa, he's the best I never
had.
His strength and his will, the courage he
showed,
Inspire my efforts and lighten my load.

Can you hear me now, in that realm so high?
Do my words reach you beyond the sky?
I'd tell you of life, the highs and the lows,
Of moments we missed, and love that still
grows.

If Heaven had cell phones, I'd call every day,
To bridge the vast distance in my own way.
I'd send you my love, my wishes, my prayers,
A connection unbroken, despite Heaven's stairs.

Can you hear me now, as I softly speak?
In dreams and in whispers, it's you that I seek.
Though distance and time may keep us apart,
Your voices still echo deep in my heart.

Perception

In the mirror of my mind, I see
A shifting form, not truly me,
A chameleon in a world so grand,
Altering hues to understand.

I've walked the tightrope, played the part,
Changed my skin, concealed my heart,
Known as brother, son, and kin,
Yet never as myself within.

Husband, father—titles claimed,
But in their light, I'm not named,
For acceptance, a fleeting ghost,
A shadowed friend I seek the most.

Whispers say I'm one of them,
Yet I stand outside the gem,
A crystal clear but fragile view,
They call me friend, but is it true?

In crisis, they appear, a flash,
To catch me as I break and crash,
But where are they when skies are clear,
When triumph wipes away the tear?

Success, it seems, a lonely path,
A silent road where echoes laugh,
For in the light, I stand alone,
A victory to call my own.

Perception shifts, a foggy veil,
Through joy and sorrow, I inhale,
The essence of my own belief,
Beyond the realm of transient grief.

I am the change, the core within,
The steady flame, the hidden kin,
In acceptance of my soul's decree,
I find the friend I've sought in me.

The Axolotl

Kick me while I'm down, don't ya?
Life's cruel blows, they break, they haunt ya,
But in my chest, a rhythm true,
A beating heart, I'll push on through.

Like axolotl, small yet mighty,
Limbs regrown, it keeps on fighting,
Though life may tear and pull apart,
Resilience lives within the heart.

When hope seems lost, dreams fade to dust,
And every step feels like unjust,
Remember, deep within, a beat,
A constant sound, a steadfast heat.

Through darkest nights and stormy seas,
Like axolotl, we find ease,
Adapt and overcome, we rise,
Beneath the weight, we still surprise.

Though shadows loom and spirits tire,
Within us burns a quiet fire,
The world can break, can tear and sting,
Yet hear the heart, its song will sing.

Kick me while I'm down, it's true,
But watch me rise, as I will do,
For in my chest, a pulse remains,
A lifeline through life's hardest chains.

Adapt, overcome, as we've always done,
In every loss, a new fight won,
Like axolotl's grace, we mend,
In every scar, we find a friend.

The Man I See

In the mirror, a man stares back at me,
Broken, beaten, and worn thin,
Dark circles beneath tired eyes,
Frayed curls in disarray, where to begin?

Since childhood, society's cruel jest,
"Funny colored kid," never fitting in,
"Not black enough," their voices pressed,
An endless struggle, a battle within.

Years spent trying to mold and bend,
To fit into places I never belonged,
Acceptance now a reluctant friend,
Revealing truths I've known all along.

The man I see has a heart so vast,
Overflowing with empathy, deep and true,
Though words may falter, intentions last,
In every act, a kindness grew.

At times, it feels my worth is weighed,
By the money I offer, what I can provide,
But true friendship can't be bought or swayed,
By wealth alone, love cannot hide.

Though beaten down by relentless strife,
A spark remains, a resilient flame,
The man I see, in this mirror of life,
Clings to hope, despite the shame.

Frayed curls and weary eyes tell a tale,
Of battles fought and dreams pursued,
In a world where fitting in often fails,
A spirit unbroken, strength renewed.

The man I see, though scarred and torn,
Carries a heart that still believes,
In love, in light, a new day's morn,
A soul that gives, a soul that grieves.

Despite society's unjust decree,
Marking me with deep, unseen scars,
The man I see will always be,
A beacon of light, a shining star.

Look beyond the surface and see,
Not just the pain, but resilience too,
A heart that yearns to be free,
A soul that's steadfast, through and through.

As you gaze into my eyes and see,
Reflecting on this mirrored plea,
Look deeper, truly understand me:
What man do YOU see?

Unbroken Ranks

In uniforms of valor, we stood side by side,
Brothers and sisters, with unbreakable pride.
From distant fields to battles at home,
Our bonds remain, though the war zone has
grown.

For every 22 a day, whose spirits seem lost,
The weight of their struggles, a heavy cost.
Today, I was nearly one of those souls,
Burdened by demons, beyond my control.

But in a moment of darkness, I reached out,
A cry for help, silencing my doubt.
Surrounded by love, my comrades in arms,
Reminded me of strength in their steadfast
charms.

In the silence of night, when shadows loom
large,
We fight a new battle, no longer in charge.
Yet with each other's backs, we stand strong,
Brothers and sisters, where we all belong.

For the battle isn't over, though we've come
home,

We march together, never alone.
With every cry for help, answered with care,
We prove that love and hope are always there.

Out Of Gas

In a world so vast and cold, I drive,
Hoping for a hand, to feel alive.
Years of struggles, roads alone,
Nine years spent, my family grown.

Family courts, like potholes deep,
Nine years of fights, dreams they keep.
A wife and two children, a journey shared,
But cracks appear where hope once fared.

I've done all I could, but fuel runs low,
Life's a mess, and troubles grow.
Every blow, a nail in tire,
Leaving scars, my path grows dire.

Imperfect, flawed, but heart so true,
I gave my all, yet none withdrew.
Eyes watched me falter, gave no cheer,
I drove alone, consumed by fear.

Perplexed, I am, for all I've done,
The father's role, my engine run.
Yet punished for trying, for doing better,
As if my efforts don't even matter.

In an economy where dreams run dry,
Fear's a constant, clouds my sky.
All I had was my work, my drive,
But even that, I can't survive.

Now I sit, watch it all collapse,
Heart heavy with the weight of maps.
Too late for hands to guide me through,
Asking for help was too much, too true.

Aches of avoidable grief, profound,
In silence, my soul spins round.
My heart aches with the weight of the past,
My tank is empty, I'm out of gas.

What Would Martin Do?

In 2024, the echoes sound,
Of a dream once voiced, a truth profound.
Invisible wounds, the silent cries,
In men's hearts where sorrow lies.

A man once stood with words of peace,
"Let freedom ring," his timeless plea.
But here we stand, still grappling,
With shadows cast by silent grief.

Brothers face a world unkind,
Where strength means silence, pain confined.
Their struggles hidden, fears repressed,
In battles fought with hearts distressed.

What would Martin do, we ask,
To lift the veil, unbind the mask?
He'd march with love, relentless grace,
To heal the hurt, embrace the race.

He'd speak of courage, bold and true,
A beacon for the many who,
In darkness dwell, in shadows fear,
With words to comfort, bring them near.

He'd stand with those who feel alone,
And build a bridge to lead them home.
With every word, with every deed,
He'd plant a hope, a sacred seed.

For in this fight, we're not alone,
His spirit guides us, leading home.
To where no stigma marks our worth,
To where all men can find rebirth.

In 2024, we ask anew,
What would Martin have us do?
He'd urge us onward, through the night,
To chase the dawn, to seek the light.

I'm Not Wrong

Would you be angry if I told you the truth,
That the world around me, in its ruthless pursuit,
Breaks my spirit with a broken economy's song,
And corrupt state hands that have done me
wrong?

Would you be angry to know I'm tired inside,
Hearing "Think of your wife and kids" as I bide
My time in a battle against endless despair,
While they are the reason I continue to care?

Each dawn brings a fight with shadows deep,
Their echoes haunt even my sleep.
But in the darkest moments, a spark ignites,
My family's love, a beacon in the nights.

For them, I endure, I strive, I fight,
Even when the world pushes me to the edge of
night.
Their love is my strength, my guiding light,
In a world that feels so wrong, they make it
right.

Translated Truth

"I'm fine," I say, with echoes of the past,
Since '15, in courtrooms' shadows, I've been
cast.
My ex-girlfriend's spite, a wound so deep and
raw,
Alienated from my firstborn at birth, a cruel
straw.

Forced to pay for a child not meant to be mine,
Yet his mother fails him, time after time.
Corruption breeds where justice should prevail,
In family courts, the truth seems all but frail.

DCF, a name that haunts my nights,
Their heavy hand has dimmed my inner lights.
They've made my life a hell, a twisted scene,
Yet still, I lie, and say I'm fine, serene.

"Living the dream," I utter with a sigh,
Yet daily, at work, I fight to just survive.
Harassment's sting and discrimination's glare,
I struggle for fair pay and treatment fair.

In this land of promise, I question why,
My efforts met with prejudice and lie.

Each day a battle in a weary stream,
In this harsh dream, where justice seems a
dream.

"I'm alright," I claim, though inside I'm torn,
No control at home, my spirit worn.
I fear I'm failing at this "Daddy" role,
Doubt creeps in, it weighs upon my soul.

My heart aches, unsure if I'm enough,
In a world that's cold, unkind, and tough.
Yet still, I smile, and say I'm doing fine,
Hiding the pain, pretending all is mine.

"Great," I respond, with a heavy heart disguised,
Expected strength, yet turmoil in my eyes.
Supposed to lead, be strong, and never fall,
But inside, I'm crumbling, standing small.

Maintaining happiness seems out of reach,
Struggling to grasp what lessons I should teach.
In the depths of night, I silently grieve,
Hoping my facade, my children won't perceive.

"Well, I'm here," I whisper, facing stark truth,
Financial woes, a system so uncouth.
Lost in the maze of bills and endless debt,
Dreams deferred, a future not yet set.

Trying to find myself amidst the fray,
In a world that's bent, where I've lost my way.
Yet here I stand, despite the odds I face,
Finding strength in each small, resilient grace.

"I'm OK," I mumble, overwhelmed and tense,
Sensory overload, my mind's defense.
Trying to express, dismissed and talked down,
Like a child, my concerns wear a frown.

Overstimulated, lost in the noise,
Seeking solace, yearning for poise.
In this chaotic dance, I strive to find peace,
In the turmoil, where emotions increase.

There's a translated truth in each word I say,
A deeper meaning, if you listen today.
Behind the mask, behind the veil,
Lies a story of strength, of resilience, unveiled.

So ask me again, and take the time to hear,
Beyond the surface, where truth is clear.
In the struggles and triumphs, the highs and
lows,
My journey unfolds, a life that grows.

Through My Eyes

I wish the world could see through my eyes,
The silent storms and the midnight cries.
Battles I face, though hidden from view,
A life-or-death struggle, if only they knew.

To some, it's a whisper, a fleeting thought,
But to me, it's a tempest, a battle hard-fought.
Each day is a climb, an uphill fight,
To find a glimmer in the darkest night.

They say, "Just smile, it will be alright,"
But they can't see the demons I fight.
The weight of the world rests on my chest,
A constant struggle, a never-ending test.

If only they saw the world as I do,
The labyrinth of thoughts I must push through.
Every step forward, through haze and despair,
Hoping for someone who genuinely cares.

This isn't just a phase, a passing storm,
It's a life-or-death battle, taking every form.
Mental health, a silent plight,
Yet it's as real as day, as dark as night.

I wish they could feel the weight I bear,
Understand my pain, my silent prayer.
Through their eyes, it might seem small,
But through mine, it's an endless call.

To those who listen, who truly see,
Thank you for being the light guiding me.
If only the world saw the battles I fight,
Through my eyes, they'd see the need for light.

So, walk with me, in my shoes, for a while,
See the world as I do, mile by mile.
For though my struggles may seem small to you,
Through my eyes, they're the battles I must get
through.

Forecast Of Feelings

On Monday, I rise with the dawn,
Bright as the sun, my worries are gone.
Laughs erupt from dad jokes so bad,
You'd think it's the best fun you ever had.

Tuesday's a sprinkle of focused delight,
With tasks and plans all within sight.
Yet, lingered in moments of quiet grace,
A hint of a smile lights up my face.

By Wednesday, clouds gather round,
A storm in my mind, I feel quite down.
Darkness encroaches, my mood is gray,
I'm trying my best to keep it at bay.

Thursday, a breeze of hopeful cheer,
Washes away the remnants of fear.
I'm buoyant, I'm bright, a wave of relief,
Turning over a new, optimistic leaf.

Friday, oh Friday, my spirit takes flight,
The weekend ahead, everything feels right.
Joy spreads like wildfire, I dance in the sun,
The happiest alive, ready for fun.

Saturday dawns with a whimsical flair,
Life's a carnival, I haven't a care.
Yet moments of stillness might shadow the light,
Reflecting on sorrows that visit at night.
Sunday's a blend, both bitter and sweet,
With laughter still echoing, sadness discreet.
A whirlwind of feelings, a forecast unplanned,
Just know that I'm moody, but doing the best I
can.
So here is my week, a spectrum of me,
From joyous to somber, I let it all be.
Emotions like weather, forever in flow,
Understand my heart as I let these days show.

Fractured Minds

If mental health were broken bones,
Each fracture plain to see,
Our hearts laid bare, our minds disowned,
No hiding misery.

With crutches for our fractured souls,
And casts for wounded thoughts,
The burdens that the darkness tolls,
In clear, stark lines would cross.

If mental health were broken bones,
Compassion would abound,
No whispers hushed, no silent groans,
Just healing, strong, profound.

We'd mend with care, each shattered piece,
In daylight, not disguise,
With gentle hands, we'd find release,
And soothe the weeping eyes.

If mental health were broken bones,
We'd treat with tender might,
And in the open, not alone,
Would find our way to light.

Daddy's Trying

Every morning before dawn breaks, I rise to face
the day,
With tired eyes and heavy heart, I pave our
family's way.
The weight upon my shoulders, the burdens that
I bear,
Are carried with a steadfast love, a father's silent
prayer.

I labor through the hours, each moment filled
with strain,
For every dream and hope you hold, I work
through every pain.
From sunrise to the evening's fall, my hands are
never still,
Providing for our little world, with every ounce
of will.

I forgo my own desires, and set my needs aside,
To build a future strong and bright, to be your
constant guide.
Through sleepless nights and endless days, I
strive to do my best,
To give you all the things you need, to grant you
peace and rest.

You may not see the sacrifices, the struggles
deep within,
The countless times I've fallen down, and had to
start again.
Each step I take, each tear I hide, is done for
love of you,
A father's heart that never quits, though
weariness accrues.

When you see me at my weakest, when strength
begins to fade,
Remember all the battles fought, the price that
has been paid.
For every smile upon your face, each laughter,
pure and sweet,
Is worth the toll upon my soul, the wear upon
my feet.

Daddy's trying, always trying, through storms
and endless rain,
To shield you from the hardships, to take away
your pain.
In moments where I falter, when courage starts
to bend,
Know that every tear I shed is one I cannot
mend.

So when you see me weary, with shadows in my
eyes,
Understand the love behind the silent, heartfelt
sighs.
I give my all for family, no matter what it takes,
Enduring all the heartaches, for the happiness it
makes.

Forgive me when you see me crying, but
sometimes it's all too much,
A father's strength can falter, in need of gentle
touch.
Yet know in every teardrop, my love is undying,
For you, my child, I'll always be, a father who is
trying.

Boys Don't Cry

Boys don't cry, they say, stay strong,
Hide the hurt, where they belong.
But hearts grow heavy, minds do break,
In silence, the soul does ache.

Behind the mask, beneath the guise,
We bury truths, where darkness lies.
Yet strength isn't silence, it's to share,
To speak the pain we silently bear.

In speaking out, we find release,
A bond of courage, a path to peace.
Together, we stand, hand in hand,
Facing fears, we make a stand.

So let the tears flow, let them be,
In vulnerability, we find the key.
For in truth and in being true,
Boys don't cry, but real men do.

Red Angels

In the quiet of my backyard space,
Where worries fade and time finds grace,
I sit alone, the world at bay,
And watch the dance of light and day.

A gentle breeze upon my face,
Whispers secrets, leaves no trace,
And in this moment, pure and still,
My heart begins to softly fill.

For from the branches, red as flame,
Two cardinals, like spirits, came,
In perfect harmony, side by side,
Their presence felt, their wings so wide.

They speak of love from realms above,
Of spirits sent on wings of dove,
To comfort those who need to know,
That they are watched, they're not alone.

These cardinals, a sign so clear,
That those I've lost are always near,
In every flutter, every song,
They bring me peace, where I belong.

Together always, never apart,
They soothe the ache within my heart,
And as they flit from tree to tree,
I feel their love surrounding me.

In their bright feathers, I see a sign,
That Heaven's touch is truly mine,
A message from the ones I miss,
A gentle, everlasting kiss.

So in my backyard, I sit and wait,
For these red angels at Heaven's gate,
And when they come, my soul takes flight,
In cardinals of comfort, I find light.

The Vindicated Vow

Amidst the shadows, in the deepest night,
I've walked through valleys, devoid of light,
But here I stand, resilient and strong,
A testament that I still belong.

Survival's a gift, a precious gleam,
In a world where not all can dream,
I've faced the storms, I've braved the fray,
And I live to see another day.

Through trials fierce and battles fought,
I've learned the lessons life has taught,
To rise again, no matter the fall,
To stand tall, despite it all.

For family, who've held me tight,
In darkest hours, they've been my light,
And for myself, I've found the way,
To turn my pain to brighter days.

Now as an advocate, I find my voice,
In sharing my story, I make my choice,
To be a beacon, to guide and show,
That none of us are ever alone.

Through my words, I hope to reach,
Those who struggle, and gently teach,
That within them lies a spark so bright,
To lead them through the darkest night.

This journey's path is fraught and long,
Yet together, we are strong,
For in each heart, a warrior lies,
And together, we shall rise.

So here I stand, my story spun,
My journey to advocacy has just begun,
To inspire hope, to spread the flame,
And remind the world, we are the same.